EDWARD P.

CW01647800

THE

MYSTERY OF HAMLET

Elibron Classics
www.elibron.com

Elibron Classics series.

ISBN 1-4021-4757-0 (paperback)
ISBN 1-4212-7621-6 (hardcover)

This Elibron Classics Replica Edition is an unabridged facsimile of the edition published in 1881 by J. B. Lippincott & Co., Philadelphia.

THE MYSTERY OF HAMLET.

AN ATTEMPT TO SOLVE AN OLD PROBLEM.

BY

EDWARD P. VINING.

"You would pluck out the heart of my mystery."

PHILADELPHIA:

J. B. LIPPINCOTT & CO.

1881.

TO

HORACE HOWARD FURNESS,

BY WHOSE UNRIVALLED

VARIORUM EDITION OF SHAKESPEARE

ALL AMERICA IS HONORED,

AND TO WHOSE WORK THE WRITER IS INDEBTED FOR THE QUOTATIONS PRESENTED IN SUPPORT OF HIS VIEWS,

THIS ESSAY

IS RESPECTFULLY DEDICATED.

PREFACE.

The views set forth in this little work not only suffer from the lack of literary experience upon the part of him by whom they are presented, but they are in themselves so different from those which have usually been held in relation to the character of Hamlet, that but little favor can be hoped for them. That most will pass them by in silence, and that some will crush them beneath the weight of their scorn, may be expected. No theory could offer a more inviting target for the shafts of ridicule; none could, at first sight, seem more absurd.

If true, why has no one seen the truth before? Who can tell! The art of Shakespeare was used to reveal the character yet conceal its real nature. Many have seen something of the truth, but stopped just short of discovery. All have recognized the human character of Hamlet, and yet all have failed to discern the true type of that humanity through the disguises by which it was clothed.

The new may be true. Even that which at first seems an absurdity may, upon investigation, prove to be the sober reality. It is something to see, or to believe that one sees, the path that Shakespeare followed,—to observe how difficulties were met,—how, with the growth of his power, he learned to substitute Hamlet's inherent personality as the origin of the prolongation of the movement of the drama, for the extraneous events which, in its earlier form, were the causes of the delay. It is something to watch his dalliance with an idea at first forced upon him, and then fondled with delight; to see with what skill he removes that which is incompatible with this cherished conceit; to note the delicate touches by which he allows glimpses of the fancy to be shown, and yet the ingenuity with which it is kept hidden.

If this patient laborer, recasting his work with loving, tender care, and moulding into it his most precious imagination, be not Shakespeare, but only the creation of a dream, then to him to whom the vision can come the dream has all the reality and pleasure of truth.

Assuming the theory to be absolute truth, there are many to whom it would be but foolishness. It is not to be supposed that those, for instance, who, in reading the tragedy, can blindly stumble over a series of careful disclosures of the length of time covered by its action, and find no clue thereto, can see a truth which Shakespeare has used all his art to conceal.

There are many who would like to like these immortal dramas and who are ignorant of their failure; many who criticise their perfections with as little appreciation as Bottom had for fairies' fare; many to whom oats and hay are sweeter than the ambrosia of the gods.

Therefore, reader, smile with disdain or laugh in ridicule if to you it seem good. The fault may be in the writer, or it may be in you. Who shall decide? If for you the following pages contain no truth, open no new insight into the mind of the world's great poet, then they are not for you. They are for those only, be they many or few, to whom they contain a revelation.

EDWARD P. VINING.

OMAHA, NEBRASKA, July 3, 1881.

CONTENTS.

CHAPTER I.

THE EXISTENCE OF A MYSTERY.

CHAPTER II.

THE HISTORY OF THE STORY.

CHAPTER III.

DIFFERENT VERSIONS OF THE STORY.

THE MYSTERY OF HAMLET.

CHAPTER I.

THE EXISTENCE OF A MYSTERY.

As among the myriads who, since the days of Homer, have attempted to crystallize in human words the ever-varying tales of human life and love, one stands out pre-eminent and incomparable, so among his works there rises one, the undisputed crown of all, with an irresistible fascination, attracting even those to whom the language in which it was written is an unknown tongue.

With an incredible plot, and a hero who, weak and vacillating, continually does those things which he ought not to do and leaves undone those things which he ought to have done, there is yet revealed a depth of human feeling, and a knowledge of the inmost springs that move the puppets whom we call mankind, before which humanity bows.

With other writers, their characters are frequently but embodied qualities, moved by one emotion. The heroine is the embodiment of love, and lives but to love, alone. The good are supernaturally good, with scarcely one contrasting vice, and the villains are creatures of crime whom no remorse can reach. One character is the embodiment of avarice; another, of ambition; a third, of revenge; and each stalks through his mimic life inspired by but a single motive. In Shakespeare's works alone do we see that tangled web of which human lives are composed: weakness and strength combined; light and shade; a thousand conflicting motives in inextricable confusion, driving their victim to and fro; and among them all we see the man, a creature of as marked individuality, as complete in his humanity, as the fellow-beings among whom we move. Other authors reveal the man by his actions, but Shakespeare shows the man in spite of his actions; and in the character of Hamlet we have a bundle of contradictions, as yet inexplicable and mysterious. No man has fathomed the depths which could produce a Hamlet. Weak and vacillating as he is, there is yet some quality which forbids that any should despise or condemn him. Macbeth, with far less of irresolution, is contemptuously dismissed as weak, yet Hamlet, constantly driven by the circumstances that surrounded him, and never able to conquer them even to the moment when they bring about his revenge and simultaneous death, commands a universal sympathy and admiration. Why should Hamlet have faltered?—why feigned madness?—why needlessly tortured the young girl who loved him, and driven her from him with coarse and cruel words? Why, in any and all his actions, should they have been as they were? Who knows?

One thing only is sure, that the character of Hamlet reveals a depth of humanity which all earnest students infallibly recognize. Like a distant landscape seen through a cloud of smoky, heated air, each particular point when steadily looked at seems to waver and flicker and be uncertain, and yet through this changing uncertainty as to details can be seen the outlines of a noble view.

What is it that so distinguishes Hamlet from all other creations of the poet? That some mystery lurks in the subtle fascination is undeniable. Of the hundreds who have discussed the subject, scarcely one has failed to note it. The following quotations will show how universal is this feeling:

"Hamlet himself has caused more of perplexity and discussion than any other character in the whole range of art. The charm of his mind and person amounts to an almost universal fascination; and he has been well described as a 'concentration of all the interests that belong to humanity.' I have learned by experience that one seems to understand him better after a little study than after a great deal; and that the less one sees into him the more apt one is to think he sees through him; in which respect he is indeed like nature herself. One man considers Hamlet great, but wicked; another good, but weak; a third, that he lacks courage, and dare not act; a fourth, that he has too much intellect for his will, and so reflects away the time of action; some conclude his madness half genuine; others, that it is wholly feigned. Doubtless there are facts in the delineation which, considered by themselves, would sustain any one of these views; but none of them seem reconcilable with all the facts taken together. Yet, notwithstanding this diversity of opinions, all agree in thinking of Hamlet as an actual person. It is easy to invest with plausibility almost any theory respecting him, but very hard to make any theory comprehend the whole subject; and while all are impressed with the truth of the character, no one is satisfied with another's explanation of it. The question is, why such unanimity as to his being a man, and at the same time such diversity as to what sort of man he is? . . . After all, it must be confessed that there is a mystery about Hamlet which baffles the utmost efforts of criticism."—*Hudson*.

"The mystery, the baffling, vital obscurity of the play, and in particular of the character of its chief person, make it evident that Shakespeare had left far behind him that early stage of development when an artist obtrudes his intentions, or, distrusting his own ability to keep sight of one uniform design, deliberately and with effort holds that design persistently before him. . . . Hamlet might have been so easily manufactured into an enigma, or a puzzle; and then the puzzle, if sufficient pains were bestowed, could be completely taken to pieces and explained. But Shakespeare created it a mystery, and therefore it is forever suggestive; forever suggestive, and never wholly explicable."—*Prof. Dowden*.

"Polonius, after a remarkable display of Hamlet's 'antic disposition,' says: 'though this be madness, yet there is method in't.' Is it possible for us to discern this 'method'? Can we discover any deeper meaning lying beneath what is outwardly so 'odd' and 'strange'?"—*Thos. Tyler*.

"This enigmatical work resembles those irrational equations, in which a fraction of unknown magnitude always remains, that will in no manner admit of solution."—*A. W. Schlegel*.

"There is no drama, as all the world knows, upon which so much has been written as Shakespeare's *Hamlet*. . . . A critical tower of Babel of amazing height and breadth has been reared, and for the same purpose as in the Scripture: to scale celestial heights. and, as people see, with the same result. The celestial heights remain unscaled."—*Klein.*

"How was it possible that a finely-cultured man, the same man whose incomparable advantages we have just been considering, an honored prince, the offspring of an heroic king, a member of the regal court, could take upon himself the shame of a disordered brain? Here there certainly lies before us a riddle which we strive in vain fully to solve, the secret of a soul into whose abyss only the greatest of poets was able to look."—*Hermann Freiherr von Friesen.*

"In the endeavor to solve the mystery of Hamlet, the human mind, not only in its clear radiance but in the sad twilight of its eclipse, has been subjected to the most searching analysis. This ideal character, Hamlet, has been assumed to be very nature, and if we fail to reach a solution of the problem which it presents, the error lies in us and in our analysis; not in SHAKESPEARE."—*Furness.*

The solution which Goethe proposed for this universally admitted mystery has been the one usually accepted:

"To me it is clear that Shakespeare sought to depict a great deed laid upon a soul unequal to the performance of it. In this view I find the piece composed throughout. Here is an oak-tree planted in a costly vase which should have received into its bosom only lovely flowers. The roots spread out, the vase is shivered to pieces. A beautiful, pure, noble, and most moral nature, without the strength of nerve which makes the hero, sinks beneath a burden which it can neither bear nor throw off; every duty is holy to him,—this too hard. The impossible is required of him,—not the impossible in itself, but the impossible to him."

Yet we find it stated that in his later years Goethe did not rest satisfied with his explanation. "After all is said," he remarked in relation to Hamlet, "*that* weighs upon one's soul as a gloomy problem."

The mystery which enshrouds the character may be suggested in a query.

Why is it that with so much that seems unaccountable and strange in the doings of Hamlet, so much that is at variance with all that would naturally be expected from a man, humanity still recognizes in him a fellow-being, intensely human in all his thoughts and ways?

That Hamlet was placed in extraordinary circumstances, surroundings so far from those with which we are acquainted that even the visit of a spirit from the grave must be accepted as an actuality, may account for many strange effects, but not for all the vacillation and weakness that are exhibited by him.

Taking for granted the existence of such a mystery, the question remains as to whether a careful examination of the drama can enable us to solve it.

CHAPTER II.

THE HISTORY OF THE STORY.

The play as we now have it is substantially the same as it appears in what is known as the "Second Quarto," which was printed in the year 1604 with the following title-page:

THE

TRAGICALL HISTORIE OF

HAMLET

PRINCE OF DENMARKE

By WILLIAM SHAKESPEARE

NEWLY IMPRINTED AND ENLARGED TO ALMOST AS MUCH AGAINE AS IT WAS, ACCORDING TO THE TRUE AND PERFECT COPPIE.

AT LONDON,

PRINTED BY I. R. FOR N. L., AND ARE TO BE SOLD AT HIS SHOPPE VNDER SAINT DUNSTONS CHURCH IN FLEETSTREET. 1604.

Until 1823 this was the oldest edition known; but in that year Sir Henry Bunbury found in a closet at Barton, in a small quarto, bound up with a number of other plays, an edition of "Hamlet" bearing the date 1603, which differs widely from that of 1604, not only in words and phrases, but even in the names of some of the characters and in the order of some of the scenes, and is but little more than half as long as the later edition. It not only omits much that is found in our present drama, but contains some phrases, and one full scene, omitted in the later edition.

There can be little doubt that these differences represent a real difference in the dramas; that is to say, our "Hamlet" of to-day differs in many respects from "Hamlet" as originally written by Shakespeare. That he re-wrote and revised the play at least once is almost certain; that he may have done so several times seems probable.

There is a period in the development of nations when literary effort is turned toward the presentation of old tales in a new form, rather than toward the creation of new themes. The old stories are repeated and re-repeated in different forms, and the popular taste is more surely pleased by a variation of a well-known legend than by a new creation. The history of Sanscrit literature is a history of almost infinite variations of a few ancient myths; and even Homer did not disdain to arrange and reword and combine the tales which had been sung by generations of bards before him. In Shakespeare's time dramatic literature was in this stage of development. We know of many of Shakespeare's plays that they are but repetitions of a twice-told tale: earlier tales and dramas were re-written; most of the characters remained the same; much of the old plot was retained; but the additions and changes made by Shakespeare were enough to constitute the difference between death and life.

Others had carved statues with a skilful hand, resembling life, but cold and dead. Shakespeare touched them with his magic hand, and they sprang into life, more than mortal. Creatures of flesh and blood have struggled through their lives and gone down to forgetfulness, their children and their children's children after them have lived and loved and striven and hoped and despaired. Some have strutted with the pride of fancied success, and some have bowed their heads in misery and despair and folded their arms above broken hearts; but one event hath happened to them all: as the one died, so died the other, and there is no remembrance of them upon the earth. Their love and their hatred and their envy is now perished, neither have they any more a portion forever in anything that is done under the sun; but the creations of our immortal poet bloom with an eternal youth, and live on unchangeable amidst a changing world.

So, in the case of the drama of which Hamlet is the centre, Shakespeare took the puppets of a former creation, and breathed into them the breath of life, and they became living souls.

Hamlet and his unhappy father, the king who murdered his brother, and the queen who married the murderer, had had an existence for many centuries. In the twelfth century, Saxo Grammaticus, a celebrated Danish historian, included in his "Danish History" the earliest form of the history of Hamlet that has reached us, repeating this, with many other stories of early days, from the information that he had acquired from old tales, songs, and traditions. About 1571, Francis de Belleforest published in a French collection of "Tragical Histories," among many other stories, some original and some borrowed, the history of Hamlet, having derived the plot of his story from Saxo Grammaticus or from some intermediate writer; and there is little doubt that Belleforest's story, either directly or through some translation or adaptation, suggested to Shakespeare the foundation of his immortal masterpiece.

Although we have no sure record of the existence of our Shakespearian Hamlet before 1603, there is undoubted evidence that a drama of that name was played as early as 1589. The first allusion to it that is found was made by Nash, who, referring to the dramatists of his time, wrote,—

"It is a common practice now a daies amongst a sort of shifting companions, that runne through every arte and thrive by none to leave the trade of *Noverint* whereto they were borne, and busie themselves with the indevours of art, that could scarcelie latinize their necke-verse if they should have neede; yet English Seneca read by candle-light yeeldes manie good sentences, as *Bloudd is a begger*, and so foorth: and if you intreate him faire in a frostie morning, he will affoord you whole *Hamlets*—I should say Handfulls of tragical speaches."

From an account-book of Philip Henslowe, a theatrical proprietor or lessee, it appears that "Hamlet" was played June 9, 1594, and that it was not then new.

In 1596 a certain Dr. Lodge published a pamphlet, in which the doctor, in discussing "Hate-Virtue" or "Sorrow for another man's good Success," says that it is "a foule lubber, and looks as pale as the visard of ye ghost, which cried so miserally at ye theator, like an oisterwife, 'Hamlet reuenge.'"

A note written by Dr. Gabriel Harvey in an edition of

Chaucer which he owned, which note there is reason to believe was written in 1598, is as follows: "The younger sort take much delight in Shakespeare's *Venus and Adonis*, but his *Lucrece* and his tragedy of *Hamlet Prince of Denmarke* have it in them to please the wiser sort."

In Dekker's "Satiro-mastix" of 1602 the following phrase occurs: "My name's Hamlet reuenge: thou hast been at Parris garden, hast not?"

These facts show that during the period between 1589 and 1603 there existed a play having the story of Hamlet as its foundation, and in which there appeared a ghost appealing for revenge. In the earlier histories of Hamlet the father of the prince was openly put to death by his brother. It is only in the later drama, of which we have no account until the year in which we find a record that Shakespeare had become a sharer in the Blackfriars Theatre, that the murder becomes a secret crime, undiscoverable except by the aid of the unquiet spirit of the victim. The change was bold, and lies at the foundation of the drama. It was a change characteristic of the genius of Shakespeare, and there seems reason for believing that it was he, and he alone, who planned it.

Four years before, in 1585, a few months before he was twenty-one years of age, twin children were born in his country home, to whom he gave the names of Hamnet and Judith. The boy, Shakespeare's first son, was named after the hero of the old tale, for "Hamnet" is but a verbal variation of "Hamlet."

How long before may the young husband, in admiration of the filial affection and steadfast resolution of the prince who took upon himself the degradation of pretended idiocy (for this and not raving insanity was the disguise assumed by the hero of the ancient story) and steadily awaited the time when it should become possible for him to avenge the open murder of his father and the calumny heaped upon him by his murderer, have determined that his first-born son should bear the name? Even for his daughter there was found a name having a double connection with the story of the Danish prince; for Judith, too, took life and honor in her hand, in order by a desperate effort of weakness against enthroned strength to accomplish a mighty and sanctified purpose; and in her name of Judith there may also exist a play upon the name of Jutie-land.

When his twins were about a year old, the youthful father, with but scanty means, removed to London to better his fortune. Here we have no record of him until three years later, when his name appears as a sharer in the Blackfriars Theatre.

How did this penniless boy attain to such prosperity within three years?

Not by his ability as an actor, for our record of his impersonations names only two parts in which he ever appeared (and one of these, by the way, was that of the ghost in "Hamlet").

It seems impossible that this unknown, impoverished country youth should have been able to leap at a bound into the partial proprietorship of the theatre with which his name was connected, in any other way than by the authorship of some one or more plays of great success,—plays winning for their author both money and renown.

When Shakespeare first tried his powers as a dramatist, what story would more naturally occur to the father, struggling for maintenance for his son, as the ground-work for his drama, than the story which in his younger days had so impressed him as to induce him to bestow upon his son the name of its hero? If Hamlet were his first play, how natural would it be that, in his anxiety that it should be seen at its best, he himself should take the rôle of the unquiet spirit whose introduction forms the foundation for all the important variations from the formerly well known story, and upon the success of whose impression upon the audience depended the success of his tragedy!

This much appears certain,—that within three years after Shakespeare's arrival in London a play bearing the name of "Hamlet" had been recently produced, and had been successful, that in this play a ghost appeared crying, "Hamlet, revenge" (and this phrase seems to have so fixed itself upon the public attention that in the only two references that we have to this early play, in which any portion of it appears, these words, and these alone, are quoted in both cases), and that the author had but recently left "the trade of Noverint" to "busie" himself with the "indeauors of art." Some youthful aspirant, previously unknown to fame, had therefore bounded into a sudden renown, by the authorship of the play.

At just this time, Shakespeare emerges from obscurity, as, in some way, the possessor of sufficient money or credit to purchase an interest in the theatre, and soon afterwards we find frequent notices of him, with laudations of his powers as a dramatist.

In Stratford there lived a certain Thomas Green, who was an attorney, and was so related to the Shakespeare family that not only does his son call our immortal poet his "cozen Shakespeare," but the burial of the father is recorded in the parish register as that of "Thomas Green, alias Shakespeare." In the lack of facts as to Shakespeare's early life, is not the assumption that he may have studied for a time in the office of this relative a reasonable one, together with its natural consequence, that when he first went to London it would be as a "Noverint" or lawyer's clerk that he would first endeavor to make his way? His works are full of legal allusions, and in this very play of Hamlet his discourse with Horatio in the church-yard shows a wonderful knowledge of legal phrases, and the reasoning of the first grave-digger with his companion is but a travesty of a legal decision given many years before, of which no one outside of an attorney's office would have been likely to know, except as it might have been popularly discussed immediately after it was given, and so have come to the ears of even a grave-digger, but to be soon forgotten. There is, therefore, abundant reason for thinking that the term "Noverint" may have been applied to Shakespeare, and Nash's reference to the "shifting companions that run through every arte" is very similar to the phrase "an absolute *Johannes factotum*" applied to the poet by Robert Green in an attack made a few years later.

Who was the formerly unknown lawyer's clerk who in or just prior to the year 1589 wrote the drama of "Hamlet"?

How did Shakespeare, in 1589, within three years after coming to London unknown and in poverty, attain such prosperity as to enable him to purchase a share in the theatre?

Does not one query answer the other, and is it possible to answer either without reference to the other?

CHAPTER III.

DIFFERENT VERSIONS OF THE STORY.

ASSUMING that the "Hamlet" of 1589 was the work of Shakespeare, the question remains whether it was substantially the same drama that we now have. We have already spoken of the differences between the edition of the play which was published in 1603 and that of 1604. These differences seem altogether too radical to be explained by the theory that the earlier publication was a piratical version, taken down in short-hand or partly written out from memory from a theatrical representation of the tragedy in its present form. There is strong reason for believing the edition of 1603 to have been printed without authority, from an imperfect copy, and to have been maimed and distorted in many ways; yet no errors of a hasty copyist, or of an imperfect memory, can account for many of the differences between the two editions. No mere carelessness could turn the names of Polonius and Reynaldo into Corambis and Montano; no dull ear of an unappreciative listener could turn the stilted lines of the mimic king, in the play-scene as we now have it, into the liquid music of the early quarto.

When Shakespeare first wrote this play within a play, he filled it with beauty and with Shakespearian characteristics. Witness the following lines:

"Full fortie yeares are past, their date is gone,
Since happy time ioyn'd both our hearts as one:
And now the blood that fill'd my youthfull veines
Runnes weakely in their pipes, and all the straines
Of musicke, which whilome pleasde mine eare,
Is now a burthen that Age cannot beare:
And therefore sweete Nature must pay his due,
To heauen must I, and leaue the earth with you."

These lines are probably somewhat corrupted, but no meaner hand than Shakespeare's wrote the verses from which they were copied.

Note the beauty of the third, fourth, and fifth lines, and notice, too, how our "absolute Johannes Factotum," to whom all human knowledge seems to be but a matter of instinct, in them prophesies the truth as to the circulation of the blood in the veins and "pipes," a truth which Harvey probably did not even suspect until at least thirteen years later, and did not publicly declare and demonstrate until a quarter of a century after the publication of this quarto.

When re-writing the tragedy, our poet felt the necessity of more distinctly separating this mimic play from the body of the drama, and, by intensifying the feeling that it was a play, of so intensifying the feeling that the surroundings were those of real life. So he carefully and unsparingly pruned out the beauty of the lines and for them substituted the following jog-trot:

"Full thirty times hath Phœbus' cart gone round
Neptune's salt wash and Tellus' orbed ground,
And thirty dozen moons with borrow'd sheen
About the world have times twelve thirties been,

Since love our hearts and Hymen did our hands
Unite commutual in most sacred bands.

* * * * * *

Faith, I must leave thee, love, and shortly too;
My operant powers their functions leave to do;
And thou shalt live in this fair world behind,
Honor'd, beloved."

Is it possible that any "actor who put down from memory a sketch of the original play as it was acted, and who wrote very illegibly," or any "bad poet, most probably a bookseller's hack," who, "without any personal intercourse with the writer of these notes, availed himself of them to make up his early copy of 'Hamlet,'" and who, according to the theory that between them they, with scarcely any appreciation for the poetry or real beauties of the play, mangled our drama of to-day into the form of the first edition, could blindly mangle

"My operant powers their functions leave to do"

into

"And now the blood that fill'd my youthfull veines
Runnes weakely in their pipes, and all the straines
Of musicke, which whilome pleasde mine eare,
Is now a burthen that Age cannot beare."?

If further proof is needed that the chief differences between the first and second quartos are owing to the re-writing and careful elaboration of the drama by the hand of him who originally sketched it out in rough, many strong arguments favoring that view may be found in the "Introductory Note to Hamlet" in Knight's edition of

Shakespeare, and a careful examination and comparison of the two forms of the drama, line by line, will furnish so many proofs of the truth of this view that their combined weight seems irresistible.

We have, then, evidences that Shakespeare's "Hamlet" was rewritten at least once. Was it rewritten or substantially changed more than once? There is some reason to believe that it was recast several times, and that we have evidences of its existence in at least four different forms.

Observe that the earlier references to the play all quote the phrase "Hamlet, revenge." The inference is strong that these were the words with which the ghost first appealed to Hamlet, and that this appeal was repeated again and again, until to the popular ear it represented the burden of its mission. Could it have so done had it been a fact that in the play as originally presented the phrase did not occur at all (as in the case of our present version), and if even the word "revenge" occurred but twice in one of the appearances of the spirit to Hamlet and not at all in the other? May it not have been that, when the history was first written, the mission of the ghost was exclusively to invite to vengeance and the burden of its appeal was nothing but "Hamlet, revenge," and that with the riper experience of Shakespeare's later years and his deeper insight into human nature he infused more of a mixture of human feelings into the yearnings of the "perturbed spirit," so as more surely to strike responsive chords in human hearts?

In our present masterpiece it is not a desire for revenge that is the main cause of the perturbation of the troubled soul. The fires in which he was confined to fast had purged and burned away not only his foul crimes but many unsanctified passions, and the yearning for revenge, merely as revenge, is but weak. It is partly a longing for the sympathy of his only child to aid him in the sufferings through which he is passing—sufferings greater than may be revealed to ears of flesh and blood—that causes him thus to revisit the glimpses of the moon; but far more than this, it is a yearning solicitude for his wife, for whom his "love was of that dignity that it went hand in hand even with the vow he made to her in marriage," to whom he was so loving "that he might not beteem the winds of heaven visit her face too roughly." That she should live in sin, and allow "the royal bed of Denmark to be a couch for luxury and damned incest," was the burden too great for his suffering soul,—a burden so great that even the sepulchre must ope its "ponderous and marble jaws" to cast him up again, that in some way he might put an end to this pollution of his loved one.

It is this for which he appeals to Hamlet, "If thou hast nature in thee, bear it not." And yet with what tenderness does he plead for the erring, guilty queen!—

> "Taint not thy mind, nor let thy soul contrive
> Against thy mother aught; leave her to heaven,
> And to those thorns that in her bosom lodge,
> To prick and sting her."

And in his second visit to Hamlet his words are but few other than are inspired by his tender care for her:

> "But, look, amazement on thy mother sits:
> O step between her and her fighting soul,—

Conceit in weakest bodies strongest works,—
Speak to her, Hamlet."

This is prefaced only by the words,—

"Do not forget: this visitation
Is but to whet thy almost blunted purpose;"

in which there surely is but little of the spirit of the appeal which first so fixed itself upon the public ear: "Hamlet, revenge."

There is therefore at least some little reason for thinking that neither the first nor the second quarto gives the drama in its first state. A clue to still another stage of "Hamlet" is found in a German play entitled "Der Bestrafte Brudermord, oder: Prinz Hamlet aus Daennemark" (Fratricide Punished; or, Prince Hamlet of Denmark), which there is strong reason for believing to be a free adaptation of Shakespeare's "Hamlet" in some one of its early forms. A translation of this German play is given in Furness's Variorum Shakespeare, from which a collation of the drama as there given, with the first and second quartos and first folio, shows the following striking points of difference, among others.

The curtain rises upon a prologue spoken by NIGHT, in a car covered by stars, who calls up her children, the three Furies, Alecto, Thisiphone, and Mægera, and reveals to them the story of the king who, inspired by love for the wife of his brother, murdered him, that he might possess both her and the kingdom. NIGHT calls upon the Furies to aid her in sowing the seeds of disunion, mingling poison with their marriage, putting jealousy in their hearts, and kindling a fire of revenge of which the sparks shall fly over the whole realm.

This prelude is poetical, and, with the exception of a few rhyming closing couplets, embodies all the poetry that is preserved in this adaptation. This mythological prologue is in the vein of the earlier English dramatists, and reminds us of the introduction to the second part of "King Henry the Fourth," in which *Rumour*, "painted full of tongues," prepares the way for the opening of the play. It appears to be distinctly Shakspearian, and to be the translation of a prologue with which the earlier representations of "Hamlet" were prefaced, but which was afterward dropped by the poet when revising and re-writing the drama.

There are many evidences that this German drama was adapted neither from the first nor the second quarto nor the present form of our English play, but from some other form of the story, containing some passages that appear in only one of the later editions, and probably some points that were dropped in them all, and also omitting many things that are common to them all, but which were added to the play by Shakespeare after their German translation had been made.

Polonius appears as Corambus, being, except in one letter, the same name as that given him in the first quarto. The king's name is Erico, the queen's Sigrie. Osric and the grave-diggers do not appear, but, in their place, the comic element is supplied by Phantasmo, the court fool, and Jens, a peasant, and in the scene in which the latter begs the intercession of Phantasmo and his protection at the court we seem to have a foreshadowing of the interview between Autolycus and the shepherd in the "Winter's Tale." Rosencrantz and Guildenstern appear only as two nameless attendants, or banditti, who, starting for England in charge of Hamlet, land with him upon an island and there attempt to carry out the king's orders for his death, by shooting him. Hamlet begs as a favor that he may kneel between them in prayer, and may give the signal for his death by stretching out his arms, when he asks them to aim both pistols at his side and be sure to hit him, so that he may not be long in torture. He kneels and gives the signal, and, just as the two banditti pull trigger, throws himself flat upon his face between them, so that they shoot each other.

This is a variation from the manner in which Hamlet outwits his enemies, as narrated in the history of Belleforest, and as given in all other editions of the drama, and may be a change made by the German adapters. There is one reason, however, for thinking that the change was made by Shakespeare, and that, later, he returned to the original story.

In our "Hamlet" of to-day, the division into acts is of comparatively recent date. The last scene of Act III. and the first scene of Act IV. are closely connected both in time and interest, but a long interval of time elapses between the close of Scene IV. of the fourth act and the opening of Scene V. Here it is that the fourth act should begin ; but to divide the acts here leaves Act III. very long and Act IV. very short,—less than half the length of its predecessor. Hence, to equalize the length of the acts, four scenes properly connected with the movement in Act III. are disconnected from it and tacked on to the fourth act. "Fratricide Punished," however, divides the acts at the point equivalent to the interval between the fourth and fifth scenes of the fourth act, and yet these two acts in this version are of about equal length. In our present drama the third act has been lengthened by the introduction of Hamlet's first interview with Ophelia, which, both in the first quarto and in the German play, occurs in the second act. The shortness of the proper fourth act can be best accounted for by the supposition that something has been cut out which originally filled it out to its due length, and this something appears to be the scene in the German drama in which Hamlet and the banditti are found upon the island, this scene having been at first replaced, to some extent, by the interview between Horatio and the queen, which is given in the first quarto but omitted in the later editions. These changes having made the original third act too long and the fourth too short, they have been equalized by the easy process of piecing the two together and then separating them near the middle, regardless of the original point of juncture.

Another instance of transposition of scenes is shown by the German tragedy, in which the court scene is placed at the end of the first act and after Hamlet had learned from his father's spirit the truth as to the murder; and it is this which at first accounted for the settled melancholy which so alarmed the king.

When the grave-diggers' scene was introduced, it became necessary to remove the announcement of the death of Ophelia, which in the German tragedy was made in the last scene of the play, to the end of the fourth act. In the German drama, as in the first quarto, the depth of Hamlet's apparent madness is more fully insisted upon, and is made to more closely resemble the brutish idiocy which the hero of Belleforest's narration took upon himself.

The reason for the delay in Hamlet's revenge is not found so much in the character of Hamlet as in the surrounding circumstances: again and again it is stated to be the number of guards with which the king is surrounded, and the difficulty of finding him unguarded:

"My worthy friend Horatio, through this assumed madness I hope to get the opportunity of revenging my father's death. You know, however, that my father is always surrounded by many guards; therefore it may miscarry. Should you chance to find my dead body, let it be honorably buried; for at the first opportunity I will try my chance with him."

"Unfortunate prince! how much longer must thou live without peace? How long dost thou delay, O righteous Nemesis! before thou whettest thy righteous sword of vengeance for my uncle, the fratricide? Hither have I come once more, but cannot attain to my revenge, because the fratricide is surrounded all the time by so many people."

The reason given for not killing the king at his prayers is that by then cutting him down, Hamlet would take upon himself any sins which he was about to confess.

The characteristic exclamation, "A rat! a rat!" uttered by Hamlet when he hears the listening Polonius, does not occur in "Fratricide Punished," but instead the question, "Who is that listening to us?" Here, too, Hamlet neither so eulogizes Horatio, nor so reviles and mocks Polonius, as in the English version.

The soliloquies, the introspection, the cynicism, the

irony, of Hamlet, are all wanting, and nothing of the mystery that enveils the hero whom we have learned to love enshrouds the early Hamlet.

The date of this form of the drama is fixed, with almost absolute certainty, to a period within a few years after 1589, by the fact that when, after the death of Polonius, or Corambis, the king proposes to send Hamlet to England, the latter replies,—

"Ay, ay, King; just send me off to Portugal, so that I may never come back again."

Dr. Latham was the first to call attention, in this connection, to the fact that in an expedition to Portugal, in 1589, of twenty-one thousand soldiers and eleven hundred gentlemen, eleven thousand of the soldiers and seven hundred and fifty of the gentry perished. It is this, undoubtedly, to which Hamlet refers, and the probability is that the allusion was first made very soon after the unfortunate event and while it was fresh in the minds of the people.

A striking indication that this German tragedy was an adaptation from an earlier play in a foreign tongue, which was, at least partly, translated from memory of its foreign original, is the fact that in the allusion to Roscius the actor the name is given as Marus Russig. Latham calls attention to the fact that there were two Roscii, and that Cicero delivered an oration in defence of both. One was Roscius the actor; the other, *Sextus Roscius Amerinus*, who was no actor at all. It is possible that Shakespeare, when first writing the tragedy, confused the two Roscii and gave the name of the actor as "Roscius Amerinus," and that this error was blindly followed and the name still farther confused in the German adaptation. In later revisions of the English play, the error was corrected by striking out "Amerinus." The blunder is one which a learned man might inadvertently commit, but which an uneducated man could not make, and furnishes a proof that, however or whenever the youthful Shakespeare acquired something of a classical education, he did succeed in obtaining more of an education than he has usually been given credit for.

CHAPTER IV.

THE DEVELOPMENT OF HAMLET'S CHARACTER.

TAKEN all in all, there seems to be strong reason for believing that Shakespeare first wrote "Hamlet" as one of his earliest plays, if not his earliest; that in this early version he changed the old story, by making the murder of the king a secret fratricide and by introducing the ghost of Hamlet's father to reveal the murder and urge his son to vengeance, and that the character of Hamlet was not then developed into its present consummate bundle of human contradictions or enveloped in its present baffling mystery; that nevertheless it was at first received with great popular favor, and did much to establish the renown of the young dramatist, who at that time was scarcely known to be also a poet; that at some future date, very possibly soon after the death of his son Hamnet in August, 1596, inspired to the work by a tender recollection of his child, he rewrote the play entirely, making many radical changes, and for the first time developing the character of the hero into some intimate relationship to the "Hamlet" with which we are acquainted; and that finally, in the maturity of his powers, say some time between 1600 and 1604, he took this offspring of his early genius and carefully revised and rewrote it, enlarging it to almost as much again as it was, and so leaving it at last, after some fifteen years of thought and study and repeated trials, in the perfect shape in which the world has since known it.

The strongest argument that has been produced to oppose the theory that the early tragedy of "Hamlet" was written by Shakespeare is that Francis Meres, in 1598, mentions with commendation the names of twelve of Shakespeare's plays, and that "Hamlet" does not appear in the list, while "Titus Andronicus" is included. Meres, however, did not pretend to give a complete list of Shakespeare's plays, and omits "Pericles" and "Henry the Sixth." While it would be strange if he should omit our "Hamlet," had it then been known, it is not strange that the name should be omitted from his list if it is admitted that the "Hamlet" of that day was the crude tragedy of which "Fratricide Punished" is a fair representative. When standing alone, it was striking and popular, but its first burst of popularity had long since worn off, and its glory had been eclipsed by the beams of Shakespeare's later dramas, so that Meres, when appealing to his list of plays representative of the genius of Shakespeare, could point to a dozen others more worthy of renown than this first production of his immature genius. It is an evidence of our great author's consummate powers that he could develop this first rough sketch into his crowning masterpiece.

Let it not be thought strange that the play should be revised so many times. There is much reason to believe that it was a common practice to rearrange and rewrite old plays. It appears from Henslowe's memorandum book that within about two years, from the summer of 1594 to that of 1596, no less than forty new plays were got up and acted, being an average of one each eighteen days. No inventive power could stand this constant drain or continue to produce absolutely new plays with this rapidity. We know that Shakespeare, like other dramatists of his age, thought it no harm to take plots of earlier authors, and even much of their language, and recast them into new forms. If he could improve upon the older play, then the world was so much the better for the improvement. There was not that fear of being accused of plagiarism that now exists. The improvement was the excuse, and the sufficient excuse, for the appropriation.

In the same way that the dramatists of that age felt themselves at liberty to improve upon the works of their predecessors whenever they could, they also believed in revising their own plays whenever they thought they could better them, and it appears to have been a common practice, when representing old plays, to produce them with such changes as the riper experience of the author might dictate. A number of Shakespeare's works bear evidence of such revision; and if it is thought that the number of changes claimed in the progress of "Hamlet" to its present state is beyond all precedent, the facts that "Hamlet" was probably one of his earliest works, and that it was finally worked up into his masterpiece, are sufficient to account for them all.

Every word of "Hamlet" is pregnant with meaning. The story can only be really read by a careful collation of almost numberless little incidental allusions, which, pieced together, reveal some point that careless readers, by the score, rush over and never even suspect. Even many earnest students seem to fail to catch much that "Hamlet" has to teach them, and few, if any, have so pondered over the magical pages that further study does not reveal beauties before unknown.

It is in the tale told by these delicate hints, far more than in the ground-work of the drama, that the second quarto differs from the first. This perfect art was not an inspiration, but the result of tender, brooding care, long continued, of patient trials and re-trials, and of numerous takings apart and fitting together again, until each word should fit perfectly into its place and have its story ready for him who would but listen to it. Shakespeare thought into this creation of his brain all that we can think out of it, and only something of the same patient, loving, long-continued carrying of it in our mind and heart that he exercised when evolving it can enable us to detect even the larger portion of that which he builded into it.

So much, then, for the history of our story. It remains to be seen whether a comparison of the character and surroundings of Hamlet in our received version, with those of earlier forms of the play, united with a careful study of the character in itself, and of the scenes in which he was placed, can do anything to remove the veil of mystery that surrounds him, and enable us to see him with the eyes of his maker.

The ancient story of the Danish Prince from which Shakespeare drew his first conception of our drama broadly sketches a few events,—too few by far to furnish incidents for a five-act play, to hold the boards for three hours or more.

The king is openly struck down by his brother, who is inspired by a desire for the rulership and by a guilty passion for the queen. He proclaims that he found the king about to kill the queen, and that in attempting to defend her he was obliged to put her assailant to death. His story is believed, his course is applauded, and he is invested with the crown. The queen, partly through fear of the revenge that he might take upon herself and her son if she denied his word, and partly as the result of her former criminal conduct, although she has not plotted the death of her husband, fails to contradict the assertion, and soon marries the usurper. Her son, fearing for his life and anxious to obtain an opportunity for revenging his father's murder, decides that he can best protect the one and secure the other by feigning idiocy, and therefore, to carry out the part which he had concluded to play, he rent and tore his clothes, wallowed in the mire, and went about filthy and distraught, all his actions being those of a man wholly deprived of all reason and understanding. The king, believing that his apparent madness was assumed, endeavored to entrap him by means of a young woman, but he, being forewarned by a faithful friend, escaped the snare that was laid for him. An over-officious courtier endeavored to entrap him in confidential conversation with his mother, and, like the later Polonius, was slain for his pains; and the following interview between Hamlet and his mother was closely reproduced by Shakespeare. The king, fearing to kill him openly, resolved to send him to England in charge of two of his courtiers, who took with them letters to the King of England desiring that Hamlet might be put to death. He, however, changed the letters so that his companions suffered that fate, and he returned to Denmark.

When he reached his home, he found that the courtiers, supposing him dead, were celebrating his funeral by a general carousal. Hamlet's unexpected return only provoked them to still deeper drinking, and the prince, volunteering to play the butler, kept them so well supplied with liquor that they soon were all stupefied. Hamlet then threw down the hangings about the wall, and, nailing them fast about his unconscious enemies, set fire to the hall.

Having so disposed of the multitude who had surrounded the king, and through fear of whom he had hitherto been restrained from attacking him, he now visited the chamber of his father's murderer, and slew him, with the words, "Now go thy wayes, and when thou commest in hell, see thou forget not to tell thy brother (whom thou trayterously slewest), that it was his sonne that sent thee thither;"—an expression which is repeated in the words of Richard III. when stabbing his predecessor:

> "Down, down to hell; and say I sent thee thither."

Hamlet, having so accomplished his revenge, addressed the multitude who were drawn to the spot by the burning of the palace, in an oration so eloquent and touching that all were convinced of the truth of his story and with one consent proclaimed him "King of Jutie and Chersonnese, at this present the proper country of Denmarke."

This is but a slender story to serve as the foundation of a five-act drama, and much constructive skill is requisite to continue the play through its three hours' course with a sustained interest throughout. The introduction of the ghost; of Ophelia, maddened by the death of her father; of Laertes, clamorous for revenge; of the court fool and the peasant, afterwards replaced by Osric and the grave-diggers, gives the piece its necessary length; but now a new difficulty is met.

In reading the old story, no hesitation or vacillation in the prince is apparent; events move quickly in the story, and although much delay really occurred, it does not strike the reader. The excuse that, as the king was constantly surrounded by an armed guard, Hamlet was compelled to wait for a fitting opportunity, seems plausible, until the play is put upon the stage; then it is evident that a young hero, panting with desire to revenge his father's untimely death, would "sweep to" his "revenge,"

> "And for his means, would husband them so well,
> They should go far with little."

Laertes, in the form of the play given in "Fratricide Punished," comes mildly into the presence of the king, and says,—

"Gracious lord and king, I demand of your majesty my father, or just vengeance for his lamentable murder. If this be not done, I shall forget that you are king, and revenge myself on him who has done the deed."

Later, however, in order to more fully contrast his character with that of Hamlet, he, with far less cause to seek revenge, in an instant brushes away the excuse as to the number of attendants constantly surrounding the king, and, raising a body of followers, overpowers the guards and forces his way to the presence of the usurper:

"To hell, allegiance! vows, to the blackest devil!
Conscience and grace, to the profoundest pit!
I dare damnation:—to this point I stand,—
That both the worlds I give to negligence,
Let come what comes; only I'll be revenged
Most thoroughly for my father."

The exigencies of the play, however, deny such a course to Hamlet. The death of the king is the end of the drama: hence it must be delayed until the play has run its proper length. Although the original tragedy was probably not more than half the length of that which we now have, even in this short form it soon was evident that the excuses that were given for the delay were not sufficient. Hamlet might have made an opportunity: if no better had occurred, he might at least have taken that which fortune sent him when he found the murderer at prayer. He must not seize it, however, for the play had not run its proper course, and yet he could not fail to grasp it without forfeiting the character of an earnest, loving, heroic son, consumed with desire to revenge the foul wrongs of his most foully betrayed and murdered father.

Now it is that the genius of our mighty poet is shown. He sweeps away all excuses drawn from surrounding circumstances, and places the obstacles to instant action in the character of the prince himself. How consummate is the skill which can create such a character, lacking in many of the most important elements that seem essential to a noble, princely nature, and yet so fine that all humanity is proud to own its kinship, and feels only pity for its sorrows, untinged by contempt for its weaknesses!

None other than Shakespeare would dare to make the attempt to present a hero of this stamp, or, daring, would have met with aught but ignominious failure.

It does not seem to have been the original Hamlet of Shakespeare: scarcely any of the perplexing contradictions of Hamlet's mind are met in "Fratricide Punished," and many of them are lacking in the first quarto of 1603. The real growth of the play, as it was re-cast from time to time, was mainly in the development of this character, and, to some extent, at least, it is probably true that Shakespeare wrote rather as he must than as he would. His mighty creation must have almost mastered him. Given the vital incidents of the drama as Shakespeare made them, and the character of the prince gradually evolved itself into that which we know it to be, and he who called him into being could hardly stay the process or change the result, even if he were disposed to do so.

Hamlet talked rather than acted, dallied with opportunity rather than seized it, because an overwhelming fate decreed that he was to be what he was.

CHAPTER V.

THE TYPE OF HAMLET'S CHARACTER.

As Hamlet lacks the energy, the conscious strength, the readiness for action that inhere in the perfect manly character, how comes it that humanity still admires him? Is not the answer to this query found in the fact that there are two types of human perfection, and that in just the same degree in which he was found to lack the essential qualities of one of these types, he took upon himself the perfections of the other?

When God created man in his own image, male and female created he them.

There is not only a masculine type of human perfection, but also a feminine type; and when it became evident that Hamlet was born lacking in many of the elements of virility, there grew up in him, as compensation, many of the perfections of character more properly the crown of the better half of the human race. All mankind has recognized the deep humanity of the melancholy prince, and many have been puzzled to find that they were instinctively compelled to bow before him in admiration, while still finding in him so many faults and weaknesses. The depths of human nature which Shakespeare touched in him have been felt by all, but it has scarcely been recognized that the charms of Hamlet's mind are essentially feminine in their nature.

The masculinity of Lady Macbeth has been universally admitted. With a woman's body she united the steady courage, the unyielding resolution, that are properly masculine.

Lady Macbeth and Hamlet are counterparts. Each is gifted with a mind naturally noble, but misplaced in the body through which it acts, and warped by the unfavorable circumstances by which it is surrounded. Could Hamlet and Lady Macbeth have changed characters, neither drama would have been possible. Hamlet with Lady Macbeth's resolution would instantly have slain his father's murderer, and she with his natural sweetness of mind, and disposition to drift with circumstances rather than to control them, would have lived and died with no foul crime upon her soul, to trouble her with thick-coming fancies, to keep her from her rest and wear her to her death.

Hamlet, Macbeth, and Lear constitute a trilogy of variants of one central theme,—the action of a noble soul under circumstances the most adverse to its development that can be imagined; in all, insanity is portrayed and the atmosphere of another world seems to surround the spectator.

Gentleness, and more or less of dependence upon others, are inherent qualities of the feminine nature, and Hamlet possessed both.

Woman, with less of strength to accomplish her desires by straightforward action, is compelled to bring them to pass by more of shrewdness and subtlety. Where strength fails, *finesse* succeeds; and therefore Hamlet plans and plots. His feigned madness, his trial of the mimic play, are stratagems that a woman might attempt, and that are far more in keeping with a feminine than with a masculine nature.

That Hamlet preferred to win by indirect means, rather than by driving straight forward to accomplish his end, is a peculiarity of his nature that has attracted the attention of many.

Says Dr. Maudsley,—

"Let it not any longer escape attention that the deliberate feigning of insanity was an act in strict conformity with Hamlet's character; he was by nature something of a dissimulator,—that faculty having been born in him. . . . Strange as it may seem, we not uncommonly observe the character of the mother, with her emotional impulses and subtle but scarce conscious shifts, in the individual when young, while the calm deliberation and conscious determination of the father come out more plainly as he grows older. Setting aside any necessity which Shakespeare might think himself under to follow the old play, it is in Hamlet's inherited disposition to dissimulation that we find the only explanation of his deliberately feigning madness, when, to all appearances, policy would have been much better served if he had not so feigned. But he has a love of the secret way for its own sake; to hoist the engineer with his own petard is to him a most attractive prospect; and he breaks out into positive exultation at the idea of outwitting Rosencrantz and Guildenstern, with whom he was to go to England."

Schlegel, too, notes this disposition:

"He is not solely impelled by necessity to artifice and

dissimulation; he has a natural inclination to go crooked ways; he is a hypocrite toward himself; his far-fetched scruples are often mere pretexts to cover his want of resolution: thoughts, as he says on a different occasion, which have but one part wisdom and ever three parts coward."

As woman, unable to fight her battles by force of arms, finds in the power of speech a more efficient weapon, so Hamlet, if words could kill, would have accomplished his revenge

> "With wings as swift
> As meditation, or the thoughts of love."

He himself seems to feel that this disposition to expend resolution in words is womanish, for he exclaims,—

> "This is most brave,
> That I, the son of a dear father murder'd,
> Prompted to my revenge by heaven and hell,
> Must . . . fall a cursing, like a very drab,
> A scullion! fie upon't!"

Carl Rohrbach, commenting upon this disposition, says,—

"He always talks more than is necessary: . . . At all events, he can under this mask [of madness] give free play to his tongue, and that, and not the use of his hands, suits him above all things. Were he a whole man and no weakling, and if he would go wisely to work, why does he not at least keep his mouth shut? . . . He is a weakling. When he says, 'Frailty, thy name is woman,' he might have used his own name here."

Hazlitt remarks of the character of Hamlet,—

"It is not a character marked by strength of will, or

even of passion, but by refinement of thought and sentiment. Hamlet is as little of the hero as a man can well be. . . .

"The character of Hamlet is made up of undulating lines; it has the yielding flexibility of 'a wave o' th' sea.' . . .

"He is full of weakness and melancholy, but there is no harshness in his nature. He is the most amiable of misanthropes."

Are not these characteristics thoroughly feminine?

Let us not be deceived by the plea that Hamlet does not needlessly procrastinate but merely wisely bides his time.

How clearly Bacon describes the drift of Hamlet's mind! "To seek to extinguish anger utterly is but a bravery of the stoics. We have better oracles. . . . In refraining from anger, it is the best remedy to win time, and to make a man's self believe that the opportunity of his revenge is not yet come; but that he foresees a time for it, and so to still himself, in the mean time, and reserve it."

So Hamlet, letting pass an unexceptionable opportunity for revenge, exclaims,—

> "Up, sword; and know thou a more horrid hent: . . .
> This physic but prolongs thy sickly days."

This was no horrible refinement of cruelty, but a mere make-shift to win time.

The true secret of Hamlet's dalliance lies, partly at least, in a fear of death. It was not so difficult to find an opportunity as it was certain that the king's death would immediately be revenged by the destruction of his slayer. This it is that supplies the clue to his soliloquy:

"To *be*, or not to *be*,—that is the question:—
Whether 'tis nobler in the mind to suffer
The slings and arrows of outrageous fortune,
Or to take arms against a sea of troubles,
And by opposing end them?—To die——"

The question in Hamlet's mind is whether he shall take a course which will insure his own safety and enable him to continue to live, and so "to be," or whether he shall, by assaulting the king, invite his own death, and so extinguish his own earthly being. Shall Hamlet be or not be?—that is the question with him. He sees that it is possible for him to end his troubles by taking arms and actively opposing them, but that such a course will probably be followed by his own death, and from that prospect he shrinks, and, after stating why it is that

"Thus conscience does make cowards of us all;"

he adds,—

"And thus the native hue of resolution
Is sicklied o'er with the pale cast of thought;
And enterprises of great pith and moment,
With this regard, their currents turn awry,
And lose the name of action."

The enterprise of great pith and moment which Hamlet had in view was the revenge of the foul murder done to his father, and the reason clearly given by him why he allowed this enterprise to "lose the name of action" is that

"The dread of something after death,—
The undiscover'd country, from whose bourn
No traveller returns,—puzzles the will,
And makes us rather bear those ills we have,
Than fly to others that we know not of."

This shuddering recoil from even the possibility of death has been passed unnoticed by many commentators, but has attracted the attention of a few, among them being Mr. Jones Very, who in an essay published in 1839 expressed his belief as to Hamlet's mental state in the following words:

"It is to this condition that Hamlet has been reduced. . . . He fears nothing save the loss of existence. . . . This is the hinge on which his every endeavor turns. Such a thought as this might well prove more than an equal counterpoise to any incentive to what we call action. . . . The thoughts of this soliloquy are not found to belong to a particular part of the play, but to be the spirit of the whole. '*To be, or not to be,*' is written over its every scene, from the entrance of the ghost to the rude inscription over the gateway of the churchyard."

Although the love of life is instinctive in all animate creatures, this timid shrinking from its possible loss, this resolution to bear even the murder of his father, the pollution of his mother, the theft of his crown, rather than to run any risk by attempting to end his ills, is certainly not what we should expect from a noble prince, the son of a man who did not shrink from meeting Fortinbras hand in hand in a mortal struggle. This dread of something after death it was that induced him to

"Rather bear those ills he had,
Than fly to others that he knew not of,"

notwithstanding that weariness which he suffered from the weight of the burdens laid upon him, which caused him to despairingly wish that

"The Everlasting had not fix'd
His canon 'gainst self-slaughter."

His weariness of life is shown again in his disconsolate reply to Polonius's

"My honorable lord, I will most humbly take my leave of you."

"You cannot, Sir, take from me anything that I will more willingly part withal,—except my life, except my life, except my life."

No slur is meant in saying that this half-confessed shrinking of Hamlet from the rôle that fate had called upon him to play is what we should expect from a gently-nurtured woman, rather than from a fervid young prince glowing with desire to end unequalled wrongs.

CHAPTER VI.

HAMLET'S NATURE ESSENTIALLY FEMININE.

In the impulsiveness which causes the hasty exclamation,—

"Unhand me, gentlemen;—
By heaven, I'll make a ghost of him that lets me!"

which induces him to jump into Ophelia's open grave with Laertes, which leads him to slay Polonius the instant that he sees the hangings stir, and which enables him at last to take his full revenge upon the spur of the moment and without premeditation, we see another feminine trait; and still another in that love of obtaining the advantage in a wordy warfare, which induces him to tantalize and mock at Polonius and Osric. How skilfully can he use his tongue, and how readily does he flay with it all with whom he comes in contact, save only one,—Horatio.

In his disgust at the "heavy-headed revel" of the king and his companions, in his "pretty oaths,"—"Angels and ministers of grace defend us!"—"By heaven, I'll make a ghost of him that lets me!"—"By heaven, I'll have it!"—"Yes, by heaven!"—in his fear of breaking into tears,—

"Do not look upon me;
Lest with this piteous action you convert

> My stern effects: then what I have to do
> Will want true color; tears, perchance, for blood;"—

in all, we see traits more characteristic of the gentler than of the sterner sex.

But far more strange than all these is the fact that all his admiration is for manly strength and manly virtues, while upon feminine peculiarities, upon womankind in general, and upon his mother and Ophelia in particular, he pours out all the bitterness of his detestation. Here is an anomaly almost against nature. The Creator has planted in humanity a subtle attraction toward the opposite sex, which in a man, and particularly in a man of Hamlet's age, invests all womankind with a tender charm. Each sex admires the characteristic virtues of the other and thinks slightly of its own good qualities. As in two magnets similar poles repel each other while the opposite poles attract, so in the human race this mutual attraction between opposites and repulsion of counterparts exists. This frequently makes the tie between mother and son, father and daughter, more strong and tender than between father and son or mother and daughter.

In Hamlet, however, we find an entire inversion of what we should have expected. His admiration is expended upon men and masculine perfections alone. His eulogy of man,—

> "What a piece of work is man! how noble in reason! how infinite in faculty! in form and moving, how express and admirable! in action, how like an angel! in apprehension, how like a god! the beauty of the world! the paragon of animals!"—

his panegyrics of his father,—

> "He was a *man*, take him for all in all. . . .
> See, what a grace was seated on this brow:
> Hyperion's curls; the front of Jove himself;
> An eye like Mars, to threaten and command;
> A station like the herald Mercury,
> New-lighted on a heaven-kissing hill;
> A combination and a form indeed,
> Where every god did seem to set his seal,
> To give the world assurance of a *man*:"—

and his dying appeal to Horatio,—

> "As thou'rt a *man*,
> Give me the cup:"—

show how earnest and deep-seated was his regard for a perfect manly character. This striking appreciation of masculine excellence was combined with an equally remarkable detestation of all womankind and aversion to womanly qualities. Witness his well-known phrase,—

> "Frailty, thy name is woman!"

his reply to Ophelia's

> "'Tis brief, my lord."
> "As woman's love;"

and his

> "Now get you to my lady's chamber and tell her, let her paint an inch thick, to this favor she must come."

In his treatment of Ophelia and of his mother this trait

is exhibited still more powerfully: in fact, such is the abhorrence which he expresses of their frailties and weaknesses that it irresistibly suggests the question, Is not this more like the bitterness of one woman against the failings of another, than like the half compassion, "more in sorrow than in anger," with which a man regards a feminine weakness? Is not this railing, in which he "out-herods Herod" and is ever "o'erdoing Termagant," more suggestive of the asperity with which women are thought to regard the misdoings of their sisters, than of any displeasure with which their sterner companions view the same faults?

It may even be asked of his bitter harangue against the tender Ophelia, whether it is possible that any young man of refined training and possessing any real nobility of character could so scourge the maiden whom he has at least pretended to love, whom he has but slight apparent cause so to strike down with brutal words, and who meets his bitterness only with mild and gentle replies:

> "Wise men well know what monsters you make of them. . . . I have heard of your paintings too, well enough: God has given you one face, and you make yourselves another; you jig, you amble, and you lisp, and nickname God's creatures, and make your wantonness your ignorance."

Did ever a noble youth so abuse and insult a lovely gentle girl?

The only scenes in Shakespeare which can be compared with this (and these are but feeble hints of the distrust and acerbity which are exhibited with cruel intensification in this interview between Hamlet and Ophelia) are those in which the disguised Viola, in her conference with Olivia, shows a woman's natural suspicion of that

> "Beauty truly blent, whose red and white
> Nature's own sweet and cunning hand laid on,"

and says,—

> "Excellently done, if God did all,"

and soon after adds,—

> "I see what you are: you are too proud;"

and the other scene, in which the disguised Rosalind, with a woman's frankness in relation to another woman's charms, retaliates upon Phebe for her cruelty to Sylvius by saying,—

> "What though you have more beauty,
> (As, by my faith, I see no more in you
> Than without candle may go dark to bed,)
> Must you be therefore proud and pitiless?
> Why, what means this? Why do you look on me?
> I see no more in you than in the ordinary
> Of nature's sale-work. Od's my little life!
> I think she means to tangle my eyes too.—
> No, faith, proud mistress, hope not after it.
> 'Tis not your inky brows, your black silk hair,
> Your bugle eyeballs, nor your cheek of cream,
> That can entame my spirits to your worship.—
> . . . Mistress, know yourself; down on your knees,
> And thank heaven, fasting, for a good man's love:
> For I must tell you friendly in your ear,—
> Sell when you can; you are not for all markets."

Taking Hamlet's taunts of Ophelia by themselves, it might be imagined that in this scene, as in the others just referred to, the apparently masculine railer was in reality but a woman attempting to play a man's part.

The question may be asked, whether Shakespeare, having been compelled by the course and exigencies of the drama to gradually modify his original hero into a man with more and more of the feminine element, may not at last have had the thought dawn upon him that this womanly man might be in very deed a woman, desperately striving to fill a place for which she was by nature unfitted, and, in her failure to do that which it was impossible for her to do, earning an admiration and a pity which no mere weakling, dawdling about his proper task and meanly failing to achieve it, could inspire.

It is not claimed that any such thought was in our immortal poet's mind when first he conceived and put the drama into shape: the evidence is strongly to the contrary. It is not even claimed that Shakespeare ever fully intended to represent Hamlet as indeed a woman. It *is* claimed that in the gradual evolution of the feminine element in Hamlet's character the time arrived when it occurred to the dramatist that so might a woman act and feel, if educated from infancy to play a prince's part, and that thereafter the changes in the character and in the play were all in the direction of a development of this idea. Very possibly the poet half juggled with himself in the matter. It is related of Thackeray,—like Shakespeare, but half appreciated by his own generation,—that when asked to finish the story of "Vanity Fair" by disclosing whether Becky Sharp killed Joseph, he answered, "I don't know."

So may Shakespeare have said of Hamlet. That the idea of Hamlet's femininity was in Shakespeare's mind, that he at least entertained the thought, dallied with it, and re-worded much of the drama to further develop it and remove all that was inconsistent with it, we shall endeavor to prove.

Let not the strangeness of this idea lead to its instant rejection, without consideration, but rather "as a stranger give it welcome."

Before considering the facts which more directly tend to confirm the view above suggested, it will be proper to remember what a favorite fancy it was of Shakespeare's to allow his heroines to masquerade in male attire. He seems to have had an intuitive fondness for placing his characters in the situations most foreign to their natural dispositions, and then allowing their natural peculiarities to show themselves and reveal the real nature of the human being whom he had created, in spite of all disguises and through them all.

In "King Lear," for instance, the drama, when it opens, shows us a man at the summit of human prosperity,—the king of a noble realm, surrounded by only those who hasten to do his will; with many apparent friends, and at least one true friend; with three children whom he believed to love him, and of whom at least one possessed an unsurpassed depth of true and fond affection for him; with riches and possessions so great that no more could be desired; with no want ungratified, no need unsupplied. Him, so rich, we see almost instantly stripped of all his blessings: his fair-weather friends desert him; his children conspire against him; his possessions are put away by his own hands and he is powerless to take them again; his one true friend is driven from him; his one loving child is an outcast; he himself is driven out into a wintry storm, with scarcely clothing enough to cover him and with no shelter to protect him from the tempest. Finally, even his last possession, his mind, is taken from him, and he has nothing left. The change is the greatest that it is in our power to conceive, and in this unexampled change the true character of the man is revealed.

The same genius that led Shakespeare to delight in so radical a transformation as this led him also to delight in fancying how his characters would act if called upon to fill the rôle of a person of the other sex. There is but little room for pleasure in fancying a man essaying to play a woman's part; but when the rôle is reversed a situation is created which appears to have attracted our author with an irresistible fascination, and of which he seems never to have tired. Imogen, Viola, Rosalind, Julia, Portia,—how he plays the changes on this one theme and never wearies of it! In all these, however, the disguise is but temporary: before the comedy ends each retakes her proper character; but in a tragedy the part once taken must be a life-long bondage, with no escape but death.

CHAPTER VII.

HAMLET'S LOVE FOR HORATIO AND JEALOUSY OF OPHELIA.

We have already glanced at some of the feminine peculiarities of Hamlet's mind, and have noticed not only his detestation of womanly weaknesses but also his regard for the character of a perfect man. In this connection let us recur to the affection of Hamlet for Horatio, with the question whether it is not rather the love with which a woman in Hamlet's position might have regarded him, than any mere friendship, such as may be supposed to exist between old-time fellow-collegians. It is evident that this depth of intimacy had not existed when they were both at Wittenberg; there they had become somewhat acquainted, but, from the difference in rank between the Prince of Denmark, the heir-apparent to the crown, and the fortuneless Horatio, who

"No revenue had but his good spirits,
To feed and clothe him,"

or for some other cause, their relations had been so far from familiar that Horatio had come from Wittenberg to attend the late king's funeral, and had remained about the court for some two months without having been seen by his former fellow-student. From the time, however, when

Horatio and Marcellus had revealed to him that they had seen his father's spirit, and when they together had watched for its return, we find Hamlet and Horatio almost constantly together, bound to each other by a friendship almost unequalled. Hamlet will not reveal the secret of the mission of his father's ghost to Horatio and Marcellus while the two are together, but at the first opportunity he seems to have disclosed the story fully to Horatio, alone, for the next time that Horatio appears upon the stage Hamlet speaks to him of

> "The circumstance,
> Which I have told thee, of my father's death."

In the interview between Hamlet and the queen, the former speaks of his knowledge of the king's purpose to send him to England, although there is nothing to show how he came to learn of this plan. It has been suggested that he had managed to place Horatio in some office or employment about the court, and that through him he may have learned this secret.

When Hamlet escapes from the ship in which he was being carried to England, his first action is to write to Horatio, telling him as much as is safe to intrust to a letter, and beseeching him, "Repair thou to me with as much haste as thou wouldst fly death." The letter ends, "He that thou knowest thine,"—a signature in striking contrast to that affixed to his letter to Ophelia.

In the grave-yard scene Hamlet and Horatio enter together, and the next scene opens with the words addressed by the prince to his faithful friend,—

> "So much for this, sir; now let me see the other."

It is evident that this opening phrase ends the narration by Horatio to Hamlet of the incidents that had occurred at the court since the latter's departure, including the madness and death of Ophelia. This is followed by a full relation by Hamlet of his adventures at sea. In this scene Hamlet appears almost nervously anxious that Horatio shall approve of his course. He seeks to stifle his pity for the death of Rosencrantz and Guildenstern by representing their treachery and their love for their base employment; he asks Horatio's approval of his intended attack upon the king, and apologizes to him for his assault upon Laertes.

Among the ills enumerated by Hamlet in his soliloquy, most of which were those which he himself had experienced, is that caused by "the pangs of disprized love." In the first quarto this line is lacking; in the second and third quartos it appears as "despiz'd love," which is changed in the folios to the form above given: and this change, with the delicate shade of new meaning in the new word, makes the phrase peculiarly applicable to the love that we may imagine Hamlet to have had for Horatio. Furness remarks,—

"A love that is disprized falls more frequently to the lot of man, and is perhaps more hopeless in its misery, than a love that is despised. As Corson says, 'Perhaps a disprized or undervalued love, a love that is only partially appreciated and responded to, would be apt to suffer more pangs than a despised love.' After all, this passage is merely one of the numberless puzzles in the text of Shakespeare."

Horatio did not despise the affection of Hamlet, but he

can have had but the dimmest apprehension of the depth of Hamlet's whole-hearted love and never suspected the true cause of the latter's confidence in him. Hence Hamlet could not but have felt that his love was and must ever remain "disprized."

His eulogy of Horatio in the third act is characterized by a warmth of fondness and admiration far greater than is natural between friends of the same sex:

> "Horatio, thou art e'en as just a man
> As e'er my conversation coped withal. . . .
> Since my dear soul was mistress of her choice,
> And could of men distinguish, her election
> Hath seal'd thee for herself.
> . . . Give me that man
> That is not passion's slave, and I will wear him
> In my heart's core, ay, in my heart of heart,
> As I do thee."

Then, fearing that fervor had led to protestation too strong, this evidence of feeling is suppressed with the words,—

> "Something too much of this."

Then follows an appeal for his aid in carrying out the plot by means of which he hoped to reveal the guilt of the king. In the last scene of all, the depth of affection between the two is strikingly shown. When first he feels the effects of the poisoned blade, it is to Horatio that he cries,—

> "I am dead, Horatio."

And, upon Horatio's attempt to drink the poisoned draught

that they may die together, he rallies all his failing strength to wrest it from him, with the desperate cry,—

> "Give me the cup; let go; by heaven, I'll have 't.— . . . .
> If thou didst ever hold me in thy heart,
> Absent thee from felicity awhile,
> And in this harsh world draw thy breath in pain,
> To tell my story. . . .
> . . . Oh, I die, Horatio."

It has been noticed that all who come within the range of Hamlet's tongue, save only Horatio, have reason to fear that ever-ready weapon; its lashes fall upon all alike: the king, the queen, Ophelia, Polonius, and Osric, all, by turn, writhe under its stings. Before Horatio, however, this prince, so merciless to others, humbly bows for approval.

This earnest affection for Horatio is in striking contrast to his heartless treatment of Ophelia. The time was when, perhaps, he could find amusement in trifling with her and playing at love; that it was but trifling is evident not only from his after-conduct, but from his mocking letter to Ophelia:

> "To the celestial, and my soul's idol, the most beautified Ophelia."

It is no wonder that Polonius should have exclaimed, "That's an ill phrase, a vile phrase; 'beautified' is a vile phrase." Hamlet's idea of the arts by which Ophelia was "beautified" is explained at length in his bitter raillery at her in his later interview with her. The body of the letter is but a continuation of the mockery with which it commences:

"Doubt thou the stars are fire;
  Doubt that the sun doth move;
Doubt truth to be a liar;
  But never doubt I love."

The conclusion of the king must be that of all:

"Love? his affections do not that way tend;
Nor what he spake, though it lack'd form a little,
Was not like madness."

In the scene at Ophelia's grave, there is evidence of many other feelings; but of love, none. He is stung by the knowledge that it is to him that Ophelia's death is owing, and stung by Laertes's curse upon him, but far more deeply is he chafed by the manly vigor of Laertes and his evident readiness to do instantly whatever fate may require of him. He feels that he himself has shown but scanty love for his murdered father, and has failed to fill the part that it was his duty to perform. In his interview with the players, he was cut to the heart by the feeling that the actor who

"But in a fiction, in a dream of passion,
Could force his soul so to his own conceit
That from her working all his visage wann'd:
Tears in his eyes, distraction in 's aspect,
A broken voice, and his whole function suiting
With forms to his conceit. And all for nothing!"—

had he "the motive and the cue for passion" that he himself had,

"Would drown the stage with tears
And cleave the general ear with horrid speech,

> Make mad the guilty, and appall the free,
> Confound the ignorant, and amaze indeed
> The very faculties of eyes and ears;"

while he himself,

> "A dull and muddy-mettled rascal, peak,
> Like John-a-dreams, unpregnant of his cause,
> And could say nothing; no, not for a king,
> Upon whose property and most dear life
> A damn'd defeat was made."

Again, when he sees the army of Fortinbras marching to war in a dispute about a little patch of ground which would not yield five ducats should it be sold in fee, he feels that "all occasions do inform against" him, and that he is exhorted by "examples gross as earth."

> "How stand I then,
> That have a father kill'd, a mother stain'd,
> Excitements of my reason and my blood,
> And let all sleep, while to my shame I see
> The imminent death of twenty thousand men,
> That for a fantasy and trick of fame
> Go to their graves like beds, fight for a plot
> Whereon the numbers cannot try the cause,
> Which is not tomb enough and continent
> To hide the slain? Oh, from this time forth,
> My thoughts be bloody, or be nothing worth!"

So when he sees the depth of feeling which Laertes shows at Ophelia's grave, and realizes that he would not hesitate to do whatever it might be in his power to do to revenge her wrongs, he is stung to the quick by the knowledge that, however deeply he may have felt the murder of his father, he has failed to do what Laertes would have done if in his place. As he confesses to Horatio,—

> "By the image of my cause I see
> The portraiture of his;" . . .

Hence

> . . . "The bravery of his grief did put me
> Into a towering passion."

When therefore he hears Laertes's wild ejaculations, he advances, exclaiming,—

> "What is he whose grief
> Bears such an emphasis? whose phrase of sorrow
> Conjures the wandering stars, and makes them stand
> Like wonder-wounded hearers? This is I,
> Hamlet the Dane!"

He *says*, "I loved Ophelia;" he *means*, "I loved my father, and, prate as you will, I would do as much for him as you for Ophelia."

> "Nay, an thou'lt mouth,
> I'll rant as well as thou."

All this occurs before Horatio, and it is partly the humiliation of feeling that Horatio may despise him when he compares him with Laertes, that leads to this wild outburst.

If Hamlet be considered as in love with Horatio, his treatment of Ophelia is easily explained as caused by jealousy.

According to the folio editions of the drama, which may

be considered as embodying Shakespeare's final intention, it is Horatio who brings to the queen the news of Ophelia's madness, enlarging upon all that she says and does, and thus proving that he must have spent much time with her, and have been upon terms of intimacy with her. Clarke remarks, "We think there is something exquisitely appropriate in making Hamlet's beloved friend Horatio the one who watches over and tenderly thinks for Ophelia during the Prince's absence, and brings her to his mother alone."

Upon the only occasion when the three are seen together, Hamlet carefully seats Horatio upon one side, while he himself monopolizes Ophelia, and, notwithstanding his bitter raillery of the morning of the same day against her, he now treats her with a pretence of courtesy, and engrosses her conversation. His coarseness treads upon the very verge of the license allowed by the times, and reveals anything rather than love, but to Ophelia it is a welcome change from the bitter reproaches which he had that day heaped upon her.

May it not have been to the intimacy between Horatio and Ophelia that Hamlet alludes when he says to her, "If you be honest and fair, your honesty should admit no discourse to your beauty"?

At this time Hamlet has in some way discovered that listeners are posted to overhear their conversation, and that Ophelia has lent herself to a plot to entrap him. So, in answer to her question, "Could beauty, my lord, have better commerce than with honesty?" he replies,—

"Ay, truly; for the power of beauty will sooner transform honesty from what it is to a bawd than the force of honesty can translate beauty into his likeness; this was sometime a paradox, but now the time gives it proof."

May it not be that Hamlet means here that the power of Horatio's straightforward honesty and incapacity for deception has failed to so translate her into his likeness as to make her incapable of joining in a plot against one whom she has received as a lover? His warning to Polonius seems based upon some such intimacy between Horatio and Ophelia as that above referred to:

"Have you a daughter?"
"I have, my lord."
"Let her not walk i' the sun; conception is a blessing; but not as your daughter may conceive:—Friend, look to 't."

CHAPTER VIII.

ADDITIONAL FEMININE TRAITS.

If Hamlet were so situated as to make marriage impossible, an explanation would be given of his raillery against marriage and of the light in which he regarded it. For him there is none of the sweetness and purity which unite two wedded lovers, and he

> "Takes off the rose
> From the fair forehead of an innocent love,
> And sets a blister there."

To be married, is, to him, but to be a breeder of sinners. His mother's second marriage is merely

> "Wicked speed, to post
> With such dexterity to incestuous sheets;"

and, in his interview with his mother, his disgust at the marital intimacy outweighs all other thoughts; his censure of her is evoked by that almost alone, and his words are rather those of the diseased imagination of one shut out from all possibility of marriage, than of the feelings implanted by nature in the hearts of the young, leading them to look upon a loving marriage as the highest earthly good, the culmination of human happiness.

It is hardly supposable that the course of the mother could so have affected a son, or that he would use to her such words as those we find. The reproof is rather such as one woman might administer to another.

Hamlet's feeling regarding marriage is summed up in his words to Ophelia:

> "I say, we will have no more marriages; those that are married already, all but one, shall live; the rest shall keep as they are."

His detestation of the conduct of his mother seems even to outweigh that with which he regards the king. When first he learns the truth, his exclamation,—

> "O most pernicious woman!"—

comes before that of

> "O villain, villain, smiling, damned villain!"

and this disposition seems to be well known to his father, for he cautions him,—

> "But, howsoever thou pursuest this act,
> Taint not thy mind, nor let thy soul contrive
> Against thy mother aught."

And Hamlet himself admits the same disposition to seek revenge rather upon his mother than upon the murderer, in the lines,—

> "Now to my mother.
> O heart, lose not thy nature; let not ever
> The soul of Nero enter this firm bosom;
> Let me be cruel, not unnatural;

> I will speak daggers to her, but use none;
> My tongue and soul in this be hypocrites;
> How in my words soever she be shent,
> To give them seals never, my soul, consent!"

Why should Hamlet fear that, like Nero, he might become a matricide?

Hunter, commenting upon this passage, says,—

"That the thought should arise detracts from our admiration of his character, as much as it precludes approbation or silent admission of the moral taste discovered in this play by its author. It is, besides, dramatically improper; for, in the first place, his mother had done nothing to deserve it; it is not even insinuated against her that she was acquainted with the manner of her former husband's death. Her offence was marrying again too soon, and, in addition to this, that her second husband was brother to the first. In the next place, such a deed would not only delay the execution of the high behest of the ghost, which is the main purpose of the drama, but would in all probability have entirely frustrated it; and Hamlet cannot be supposed not to have foreseen that such would be the result. Hamlet a matricide would have become instantly an object of universal odium. In fact, the truth cannot and ought not to be concealed that, popular as this play is, not in England only, but all the world over, there are parts in it which seem quite at variance with the ordinary modes of thinking of its author."

When we find faults in Shakespeare, the cause may be rather in our own understanding than in the author's conception; and if we imagine that the poet here portrayed a woman incapable of accomplishing the revenge which the perturbed spirit of her father had imposed upon her, driven to the borders of distraction by unbearable burdens, suffering from a hopeless love that she might never reveal, tortured by jealousy, sorely sensitive to all a woman's natural faults, and incensed far more at the sacrifice of personal purity made by her mother in marrying again so speedily, than even by the murder of her father; shrinking from the mortal struggle with the king, fearing bloodshed, and viewing the possibility of her own death with a shuddering horror, and hence anxious to find some escape, some easier method of fulfilling her duty; that which before seemed at variance with all our ordinary modes of thinking now becomes an exhibition of the deepest human feeling.

To pour upon another woman, and she an erring one, open to censure, a volley of burning blame, was much easier than with sword in hand to attack the king in mortal combat. Here was a task which Hamlet could do efficiently, and from this he did not shrink. Poor soul! he wanted to be firm and cruel in order to be able to carry out the ghost's behest, and his firmness, although it vanished at the sight of his uncle, could carry him easily enough through a scolding-match with his mother; but as for her life being in danger, that was but an exaggeration of his feelings by which Hamlet endeavored to deceive himself: he could strut and bellow bravely before an erring woman, and so he endeavored to screw his courage to the sticking-point and prepare himself for the bloody work which fate had ordained for him. How well he succeeded is shown by the fact that immediately after the utterance of these words—in fact, almost before they have died upon his lips—destiny gives him the opportunity for which he has endeavored to persuade himself that he has been seeking, and again his courage fails him, and he turns his back upon it, with another brave speech by which again he tries to excuse himself to his own heart.

There is noticeable in Hamlet a quickness of appreciation of difference of sex, that would indicate that the subject was one upon which his mind was often fixed. When, for instance, he remarks,—

> "And yet, to me, what is this quintessence of dust? man delights not me,"—

observing that Rosencrantz laughs, he instantly adds,—

> "No, nor woman neither, though, by your smiling you seem to say so."

Again, in his dialogue with the grave-digger, when he asks,—

> "What man dost thou dig it for?"—

and receives the reply,—

> "For no man, sir,"—

he immediately questions,—

> "What woman then?"

When Hamlet, seeing the skull thrown from the grave "knocked about the mazzard with a sexton's spade," exclaims, "Did these bones cost no more the breeding, but to play at loggats with 'em? mine ache to think on't," this instinctive thought of the cost of pain, anxiety, and danger by which they came into being, seems thoroughly feminine.

Hamlet's bodily characteristics seem to be as feminine as his mind. He was small and delicate, for he can think of no greater contrast than that between Hercules and himself, and yet was at least moderately plump, for during his fencing-match the queen says,—

> "He's fat and scant of breath.—
> Here, Hamlet, take my napkin, rub thy brows."

He has a woman's daintiness and sensitiveness to the weather and to perfumes. When he appears upon the platform, to wait for the appearance of the ghost, his first words are,—

> "The air bites shrewdly; it is very cold."

Again, in his conversation with Osric he speaks of the weather, and blows hot and cold with the same breath. When handling Yorick's skull, which had lain in the earth three-and-twenty years, he asks,—

> "Dost thou think Alexander looked o' this fashion i' the earth?"

and receives the reply, "E'en so," he adds, "And smelt so? puh!" and throws down the skull.

In the first quarto, when Osric approaches with the salutation,—

> "Now God saue thee, sweete Prince *Hamlet!*"

the latter replies,—

> "And you sir: foh, how the muske-cod smels!"

And when Osric says,—

"I shall deliuer your most sweet answer,'

Hamlet answers,—

"You may sir, none better, for y'are spiced.
Else he had a bad nose could not smell a foole."

Hamlet, too, is hysterical. Edward R. Russell, in an essay upon Irving as Hamlet, says,—

"Irving has noticed that Hamlet is not merely simple-minded, frankly susceptible, and naturally self-contemplative, but has a trick—not at all uncommon in persons whose most real life is an inner one—*of fostering and aggravating his own excitements.* This discovery of Irving is a stroke of high genius, and will identify his Hamlet as long as the memory of it endures. . . . Does Irving discard the tablets? By no means. But he makes the use of them lifelike and probable. His snatching them from his pocket, and writing on them, is the climax of an outburst hardly distinguishable from hysteria."

The faintness which attacks the prince, after the revelation of the ghost, is such as might trouble a woman:

"Oh, fie! hold, hold, my heart;
And you, my sinews, grow not instant old,
But bear me stiffly up."

So the disguised Julia faints from excess of feeling. So the masquerading Rosalind, overcome by emotion, faints, and then tries to excuse herself to Oliver:

"*Oli.* Be of good cheer, youth:—you a man?—You lack a man's heart.

"*Ros.* I do so, I confess it. Ah, sir, a body would think this was well counterfeited: I pray you, tell your brother how well I counterfeited.—Heigh ho!—

"*Oli.* This was not counterfeit; there is too great testimony in your complexion, that it was a passion of earnest.

"*Ros.* Counterfeit, I assure you.

"*Oli.* Well then, take a good heart, and counterfeit to be a man.

"*Ros.* So I do: but, i' faith, I should have been a woman by right."

Hamlet's physical strength was no greater than might be expected of a woman. In the struggle with Laertes in Ophelia's grave, he was instantly overcome, and could do no more than gasp,—

"I prithee take thy fingers from my throat."

His one manly accomplishment was the art of fencing: this requires more skill than strength, and therefore Hamlet excelled in it; and yet, with equal skill, superior strength would give an advantage, and therefore Hamlet falls a little short of the best, and needs odds in his favor in a match with Laertes.

CHAPTER IX.

HAMLET'S AGE AND BIRTH—THE TERMS USED IN ADDRESSING HIM.

HAMLET'S youthful beauty was far greater than is natural in a man thirty years of age. The impression constantly left by the references to him is that his appearance was that of extreme youth. Horatio speaks of him as "Young Hamlet," and the grave-digger repeats the phrase. He is a student fresh from the university.

Laertes speaks of his love as "a violet in the youth of primy nature." Ophelia testifies as to his grace and beauty,—

"Oh, what a noble mind is here o'erthrown!
The courtier's, scholar's, soldier's, eye, tongue, sword;
The expectancy and rose of the fair state,
The glass of fashion, and the mould of form,
The observed of all observers,"

with

"Unmatch'd form and feature of blown youth."

Nor is Ophelia alone in admiration of Hamlet. Horatio, at his death, exclaims,—

"Now cracks a noble heart."

Fortinbras testifies,—

> "He was likely, had he been put on,
> To have proved most royally."

The king bears witness to

> "The great love the general gender bear him;
> Who, dipping all his faults in their affection,
> Would, like the spring that turneth wood to stone,
> Convert his gyves to graces;"

and upon another occasion states that

> "He's loved of the distracted multitude,
> Who like not in their judgement, but their eyes."

In the first quarto there is nothing to lead one to imagine that Hamlet is more than a youth, scarcely twenty years of age, perhaps; but in the later editions Hamlet's age is fixed by the remarks of the grave-digger, and by the length of married life of the mimic king and queen, at thirty years; and yet, with this increased age (which was a deliberate change of Shakespeare's, as is shown by at least two other changes in the lengths of time named in the grave-diggers' scene, and which therefore had a purpose), Hamlet remains as youthful in appearance as before.

Is not Hamlet's extreme maturity of mind, combined with his youthfulness of appearance, notwithstanding his actual age of thirty years, strong proof that here was a woman masquerading in a manly part? A very plain-looking woman will pass for a very handsome man, when suitably attired; and the natural brightness and freshness of her complexion, combined with absence of beard, will give her a boyish appearance, making her look far younger than her real age.

It is noticeable that it is stated that young Hamlet was born the day that the last King Hamlet overcame Fortinbras,—that is to say, upon the day that the news of the combat reached the court and people. From Horatio's narration to Marcellus, in the first scene of the drama, it appears that this combat was a mortal, hand-to-hand struggle between King Hamlet and Fortinbras, in which the latter was slain. It is not to be supposed that Hamlet escaped entirely unscathed from such a contest. The presumption is reasonable that he was severely injured, and that it may have taken him long to recover from his wounds, if indeed he ever did fully recover.

News of the struggle reaches the court: Fortinbras is slain, Hamlet wounded; probably at first only half-reliable rumors are received, crowding fast upon one another, and so contradictory as to make the actual result of the combat uncertain. In the midst of the excitement and confusion the trial of the young queen comes upon her. A son had been anxiously expected. The queen knows that the successor to the throne is chosen by election of the nobles, and that no daughter could hope to inherit the crown.

Now, alone, with her husband seriously, possibly mortally, injured,—with perhaps some reason for thinking that no other child would ever be born to them (and none other ever was),—the queen gives birth to their child. If it should prove to be a daughter, the disappointment would be great. Is it conceivable that, if the expected child was found to be a girl, the queen, with the aid of one or two faithful attendants, who had died before our drama opens, could have acted upon a sudden determination and succeeded in passing the child off as a son?

This step once hastily taken could not be recalled. If it were taken, then the unhappy child must be brought up as a boy and trained to play, as well as in her lay the power, the part of the expected son whom she had replaced. There could be no retreat, no change: the part once taken must be played through to the end.

The queen's moral nature was not above this deception: that is evident from her after-career. Hamlet himself seems to have inherited much of her fondness for dissimulation, combined with much of his nobler father's disposition.

If a girl were thus educated, and if she should then be placed in the position in which we find Hamlet, is not the action of Hamlet such as we might expect from a noble woman thus unhappily situated?

If this wild imagination were true, could ever human being be more unhappily placed or deserve a deeper sympathy than the unfortunate Hamlet?

Let it be observed that the spirit of Hamlet's father never calls him "son": that word is carefully avoided, although it is doubtful whether another appeal of half the length, by a father to his son, can be found, in which the word is not used. What more natural appeal for the perturbed spirit than the yearning cry, "My son"? but it never comes.

In "Fratricide Punished," which we imagine to be an adaptation of the tragedy in one of its earliest forms, before the character had grown in Shakespeare's mind to be anything like that of our Hamlet, the ghost says, "Then hear, my son Hamlet, what I have to tell thee of thy father's unnatural death."

Is it accidental that the term is omitted in our later forms and that the ghost addresses him only as "Hamlet" and "thou noble youth"?

This is all the more remarkable from contrast with the speech of the usurper, who seldom addresses Hamlet without using that term; and at each repetition of the word Hamlet winces as if a festering sore had been rudely touched. The first words that Hamlet speaks upon the stage are in answer to the king's address:

> "And now, my cousin Hamlet, and my son;"

at which Hamlet says, aside,—

> "A little more than kin, and less than kind."

This "kind" should be read with a short vowel, as the German word for "child." It should be remembered that Hamlet had but recently returned from Wittenberg, and that the use of German words would be natural for him. Here the expression is a protest against the name of "son" which the king bestows upon him. He is a little more than kin, for he is Claudius's nephew and also the son of his wife, but he is less than his "kind" or child.

Additional proof that the word "kind" is used in its German sense of "child" is found in the use of another German word, "crants" (the German "kranz," the Danish "krands"), with the meaning "wreath," in the words of the priest at Ophelia's grave:

"Yet here she is allow'd her virgin crants,
Her maiden strewments and the bringing home
Of bell and burial."

Another protest against being called the son of Claudius is seen in the continuation of the conversation between the king and Hamlet above referred to. The king proceeds,—

"How is it that the clouds still hang on you?"

and Hamlet answers,—

"Not so, my lord; I am too much i' the *sun*."

Neither of these passages occurs in the first quarto: they were after-thoughts of the poet.

This wincing at the claimed relationship is shown by Hamlet's retaliation when he bids farewell to the king, upon his departure for England, with the words, "Farewell, dear mother." The unhappy prince finds an excuse for the phrase, but its real meaning is, "I am as near right in calling you 'mother' as you are in calling me 'son.'"

In this connection it is proper to notice the main objections that may be urged against the theory that we have presented.

Hamlet speaks of himself as a son in the following passages:

"This is most brave,
That I, the son of a dear father murder'd,
Prompted to my revenge by heaven and hell,
Must . . . fall a-cursing, like a very drab,
A scullion!"

"That would be scann'd:
A villain kills my father; and for that,
I, his sole son, do this same villain send
To heaven."

"Do you not come your tardy son to chide,
That, lapsed in time and passion, lets go by
The important acting of your dread command?
Oh, say!"

In all these passages it is plain that Hamlet speaks of himself as he would appear to others. In the first he chides himself for acting like a woman; the second commences, "That would be scanned," indicating clearly the intention to look at his case from an external stand-point; and as to the third instance it may be said that he had become so accustomed to outwardly playing a son's part that the word would unconsciously spring to his lips. In two other cases he speaks of himself to others as a son, but could hardly do otherwise, even were there no question as to the truth of the views herein advanced:

"O wonderful son, that can so astonish a mother!"

"Besides, to be demanded of a sponge, what replication should be made by the son of a king?"

Twice the queen addresses Hamlet as a son:

"O gentle son,
Upon the heat and flame of thy distemper
Sprinkle cool patience."

"O, my son, what theme?"

and the constant habit of considering Hamlet as a son,

and so addressing him before others, may well account for these. Once more, in speaking to Guildenstern and Rosencrantz, she says,—

> "And I beseech you instantly to visit
> My too much changed son,"—

and this is all. When Polonius announces his supposed discovery that Hamlet's madness is caused by his love for Ophelia, the queen answers,—

> "It may be, very likely."

Addressing Ophelia, the queen says,—

> "For your part, Ophelia, I do wish
> That your good beauty be the happy cause
> Of Hamlet's wildness;"

and at her grave she says,—

> "I hoped thou shouldst have been my Hamlet's wife;
> I thought thy bride-bed to have deck'd, sweet maid."

But, if the queen had been for thirty years endeavoring to conceal the truth, it is not strange that she should speak of Hamlet in this manner before others. It is noticeable that when alone with Hamlet she never refers to Ophelia,—no, not even when the death of Polonius would naturally lead to the question as to its effect upon her son's relations with Polonius's daughter. One further objection may be noted in the text:

> "Am I a coward?
> Who calls me villain? breaks my pate across?

Plucks off my beard, and blows it in my face?
Tweaks me by the nose? gives me the lie i' the throat
As deep as to the lungs? Who does me this?"

This reference to plucking off the beard may be considered as a proverbial expression rather than as an indication that Hamlet wore a beard. For some reason, all actors have played the part of our hero with a smooth and beardless face, and have not found so playing it inconsistent with the words above quoted. May not this be a tradition of the stage, coming down unbrokenly from the time of Shakespeare to the present day, and is not this beardless face one of the reasons for the youthful appearance of Hamlet, notwithstanding his thirty years?

CHAPTER X.

HAMLET'S HINTS OF FEMININITY—COMPARISON BETWEEN DIFFERENT EDITIONS.

In instances in which Shakespeare's heroines are disguised, they frequently slyly allude to their femininity, or drop little remarks from which clear-sighted acuteness might infer it; and there are some of Hamlet's sayings which may pass for allusions of this kind. Several of these half-hints have already been noticed, and the following are worthy of attention. Hamlet's half-soliloquy before Horatio, while they are watching for his father's spirit, seems of this nature:

"So, oft it chances in particular men,
That for some vicious mole of nature in them,
As, in their birth,—wherein they are not guilty,
Since nature cannot choose his origin,—
By the o'ergrowth of some complexion,
Oft breaking down the pales and forts of reason,
Or by some habit, that too much o'er-leavens
The form of plausive manners; that these men,—
Carrying, I say, the stamp of one defect,
Being nature's livery, or fortune's star,—
Their virtues else,—be they as pure as grace,
As infinite as man may undergo—
Shall in the general censure take corruption
From that particular fault; the dram of e'il

> Doth all the noble substance often dout,
> To his own scandal."

And his assertion to Horatio, a few moments later,—

> "There are more things in heaven and earth, Horatio,
> Than are dreamt of in your philosophy;"—

is possibly but a continuance of the same brooding over the mysterious natural fault in himself of which he first complained. His protest to his mother,—

> "These indeed 'seem,'
> For they are actions that a *man* might play;"

may possibly be an allusion of the same kind. His letter to Ophelia ends with the following remarkable clause:

> "Thine evermore, most dear lady, whilst this machine is to him, HAMLET."

That is to say, I am your faithful lover as long as my body is known as Hamlet, but if the time comes when it is found that that name is inappropriate for me and that I have no right to bear it, then you will see that I am not and cannot be yours. Just before the fencing-match which causes his death, he turns to Horatio with the words,—

> "Thou wouldst not think how ill all's here about my heart;
> But it is no matter."

And upon Horatio's hasty protest, "Nay, good my lord," —he continues,—

> "It is but foolery; but it is such a kind of gaingiving as would perhaps trouble a woman."

In "Fratricide Punished" there is a somewhat similar expression used by the queen: "I doubt much whether my heart will be at ease, for I know not what kind of an approaching misfortune disturbs our spirits." This womanly foreboding Shakespeare seems, later, to have transferred to Hamlet.

But the most remarkable hint is given in Hamlet's dying words. It is usually expected that there shall be some depth of meaning, some concentration of the soul's experience, in the last words that fall feebly from the chilling lips as the spirit abandons its grasp upon earthly things; and "last words" are long remembered. In Hamlet's case, after beseeching Horatio to live to tell his story and relate

> "The occurrents, more and less,
> Which have solicited—"

he adds,—

> "The rest is silence."

What is it that is doomed to silence? Horatio has known all that we know of the events that occur upon the stage when he is not present: it is only necessary to wait for his next appearance to see proof that Hamlet in the interim has told him all. Nothing has been hidden from him, unless it be some solemn life-long mystery, that must be carried into the grave.

Ah, breaking heart, that even in death must suffer in silence! Can it be that the seal of silence shall ever be removed? Shall human pity ever sound the depths of woe that engulfed this unhappy life?

Even in its silence it cries for sympathy. Was its burden

this,—that, being born for love and protection, it was hopelessly cut off from all earthly love, all human aid?—that, yearning for a noble, vigorous nature upon which to lean, a nature that might complement its own abundant sweetness and nobility with manly power, it was not only denied all assistance, but was compelled to stagger under a load of woes too heavy for even the strongest, and vainly try to bear a weight too severe for far greater powers? Who knows? Possibly even Shakespeare himself never fully solved the riddle which fate gradually forced upon him as Hamlet grew beneath his hand.

That the character grew to be very different from that which was intended in the beginning, and that the change was constantly toward the development of the feminine element and the pruning out of all that was inconsistent therewith, is placed beyond all reasonable doubt by a comparison of the first and second quartos, and is still further proved by a comparison of these with "Fratricide Punished," if it be admitted that the latter is an adaptation of an earlier stage of Shakespeare's drama.

It is remarkable that, of the five quotations last given, only one, "There are more things in heaven and earth, Horatio," occurs in the first quarto. Other differences between the two quartos have been already shown, and it may now be noted, in addition to these, that the following passages, all bearing upon our theory, are not found in the earlier form of the play:

> "This heavy-headed revel east and west."
>
> "Let not the royal bed of Denmark."

"Hold, hold, my heart;
And you, my sinews."

"O most pernicious woman!"

"Let her not walk i' the sun."

"Except my life, except my life."

"The pangs of disprized love."

"And thus the native hue of resolution
Is sicklied o'er with the pale cast of thought."

"The expectancy and rose of the fair state,
The glass of fashion, and the mould of form."

"For what advancement may I hope from thee,
That no revenue hast but thy good spirits?"

"Since my dear soul was mistress of her choice,
And could of men distinguish, her election
Hath seal'd thee for herself."

"Give me that man
That is not passion's slave, and I will wear him
In my heart's core, ay, in my heart of heart,
As I do thee."

"You would pluck out the heart of my mystery."

"That would be scann'd."

"Such an act
That blurs the grace and blush of modesty."

"Hyperion's curls; the front of Jove himself; . . .
A combination and a form indeed,
Where every god did seem to set his seal
To give the world assurance of a man."

"What I have to do
Will want true color! tears perchance for blood."

"Good night; but go not to mine uncle's bed.
Assume a virtue, if you have it not."

"No, in despite of sense and secrecy,
Unpeg the basket on the house's top.
Let the birds fly, and like the famous ape,
To try conclusions, in the basket creep,
And break your own neck down."

"Let it work:
For 'tis the sport to have the engineer
Hoist with his own petard."

"I see a cherub that sees them."

"How all occasions do inform against me,
And spur my dull revenge!"

"How came he dead? I'll not be juggled with."

"But, sure, the bravery of his grief did put me
Into a towering passion."

"He's fat and scant of breath."

"As thou'rt a man."

It may be observed, also, that the second quarto changes the length of the wedded life of the mimic king and queen from forty years to thirty, so as to make the time in consonance with that of Hamlet's parent's marriage; that the length of time for which the clown has been a grave-digger is also changed to thirty years, having previously been only twelve years; that Hamlet's letter to Horatio first appears in the second quarto, and that the entrance of Horatio with Ophelia is not shown before the publication of the first folio.

In the first quarto the ghost says to Hamlet in relation to his mother,—

> "Speake to her Hamlet, *for her sex is weake.*"

This is stricken out in the later edition.

The queen also addresses Hamlet with the exclamation, "How now, boy!" and this too was afterwards changed.

As a final indication of the truth of our theory, may be noted the fact of Hamlet's death. The criticism has been made, that the drama would be a more perfect work of art if Hamlet were finally allowed to execute the ghost's behest in some open and solemn manner, and then, as in the original story of Hamlet, have so explained his cause as to lead to universal belief in the truth of his claims, and to his investment with the crown, closing the drama with Hamlet left to a happy, prosperous life.

The death of Hamlet may at first have been dictated by a pandering to the popular bloody-minded taste; but in this, as in the reason for delay in fulfilling the ghost's commands, we may conclude that Shakespeare's riper powers substituted a sufficient reason in the character of the hero. Hamlet must die, for the "cursed spite" under which he was born was such that for his woes there could be no other end than death.

FINIS.

782834

Printed in Great Britain by
Amazon.co.uk, Ltd.,
Marston Gate.